To

_____

From

_____

Date

_____

*199 Favorite Bible Verses for Leaders*

© 2008 Christian Art Gifts, RSA
     Christian Art Gifts Inc., IL, USA

Designed by Christian Art Gifts

Images used under license from Shutterstock.com

Printed in China

ISBN 978-1-77036-123-2

10  11  12  13  14  15  16  17  18  19  –  15  14  13  12  11  10  9  8  7  6

# 199 favorite
## Bible verses for
# leaders

christian
art gifts ®

# CONTENTS

A Leader ...

A Leader ...

# Acts with Integrity

You must be careful how

you walk, and where you go,

for there are those following

you who will set their feet

where yours are set.

*Robert E. Lee*

**1**

"You are truly My disciples if you remain faithful to My teachings. And you will know the truth, and the truth will set you free."

*John 8:31-32 NLT*

**2**

Righteousness guards the man of integrity.

*Proverbs 13:6*

**3**

For the LORD is righteous; He loves righteous deeds; the upright shall behold His face.

*Psalm 11:7 ESV*

**4**

Light shines on the godly, and joy on those whose hearts are right.

*Psalm 97:11 NLT*

God is faithful, and He will not let you be tempted beyond your ability, but with the temptation He will also provide the way of escape, that you may be able to endure it.

*1 Corinthians 10:13 ESV*

People with integrity walk safely.

*Proverbs 10:9 NLT*

Who may ascend into the hill of the LORD? Or who may stand in His holy place? He who has clean hands and a pure heart.

*Psalm 24:3-4 NKJV*

The godly walk with integrity; blessed are their children who follow them.

*Proverbs 20:7 NLT*

**9**

You have upheld me because of my integrity, and set me in Your presence forever.

*Psalm 41:12 ESV*

**10**

A faithful man will be richly blessed.

*Proverbs 28:20*

**11**

"Blessed are the pure in heart, for they shall see God."

*Matthew 5:8 NKJV*

---

*People don't care how much you know until they know how much you care.*

John Maxwell

A Leader ...

Controls Anger

Whatever is begun in anger

ends in shame.

*Benjamin Franklin*

**12**

Slowness to anger makes for deep understanding; a quick-tempered person stockpiles stupidity.

*Proverbs 14:29 The Message*

**13**

A soft answer turns away wrath, but a harsh word stirs up anger.

*Proverbs 15:1 NKJV*

**14**

Stop being angry! Turn from your rage! Do not lose your temper – it only leads to harm.

*Psalm 37:8 NLT*

**15**

Everyone should be quick to listen, slow to speak and slow to become angry, for man's anger does not bring about the righteous life that God desires.

*James 1:19-20*

**16**

Hot tempers start fights; a calm, cool spirit keeps the peace.

*Proverbs 15:18 The Message*

**17**

Don't sin by letting anger control you. Don't let the sun go down while you are still angry, for anger gives a foothold to the devil.

*Ephesians 4:26, 27 NLT*

**18**

Set a guard over my mouth, O LORD; keep watch over the door of my lips.

*Psalm 141:3*

**19**

Knowing God leads to self-control. Self-control leads to patient endurance, and patient endurance leads to godliness.

*2 Peter 1:6 NLT*

**20**

Love is not rude, it is not self-seeking, it is not easily angered, it keeps no record of wrongs.

*1 Corinthians 13:5*

**21**

The mouth of a good person is a deep, life-giving well, but the mouth of the wicked is a dark cave of abuse.

*Proverbs 10:11 The Message*

**22**

Sensible people control their temper; they earn their respect by overlooking wrongs.

*Proverbs 19:11 NLT*

---

*Be willing to make decisions.*
*That's the most important*
*quality in a good leader.*

George S. Patton Jr.

A Leader ...

# Depends on God
# for Success

---

The history of the world

is but the biography

of great men.

*Thomas Carlyle*

---

**23**

The LORD will make you the head, not the tail. If you pay attention to the commands of the LORD and carefully follow them, you will always be at the top, never at the bottom.

*Deuteronomy 28:13*

**24**

The LORD your God will bless you in all your harvest and in all the work of your hands, and your joy will be complete.

*Deuteronomy 16:15*

**25**

The LORD will send rain at the proper time from His rich treasury in the heavens and will bless all the work you do.

*Deuteronomy 28:12 NLT*

**26**

Submit to God and be at peace with Him; in this way prosperity will come to you.

*Job 22:21*

**27**

For the LORD God is a sun and shield; the LORD bestows favor and honor. No good thing does He withhold from those who walk uprightly.

*Psalm 84:11 ESV*

**28**

With God we will gain the victory, and He will trample down our enemies.

*Psalm 60:12*

**29**

My cup overflows with blessings. Surely Your goodness and unfailing love will pursue me all the days of my life.

*Psalm 23:5-6 NLT*

**30**

Commit to the LORD whatever you do, and your plans will succeed.

*Proverbs 16:3*

**31**

"For to everyone who has will more be given, and he will have an abundance."

*Matthew 25:29 ESV*

**32**

You go before me and follow me. You place Your hand of blessing on my head.

*Psalm 139:5 NLT*

---

*Success is not the key*
*to happiness.*
*If you love what you are doing,*
*you will be successful.*

Albert Schweitzer

A Leader ...

Is Forgiving

Forgiveness is the fragrance

the violet sheds on the heel

that has crushed it.

*Mark Twain*

**33**

Be kind and compassionate to one another, forgiving each other.

*Ephesians 4:32*

**34**

"Forgive your friend. Even if it's personal against you and repeated seven times through the day, and seven times he says, 'I'm sorry, I won't do it again,' forgive him."

*Luke 17:3-4 The Message*

**35**

"For if you forgive men when they sin against you, your heavenly Father will also forgive you."

*Matthew 6:14*

**36**

"Whenever you stand praying, forgive, if you have anything against anyone, so that your Father also who is in heaven may forgive you your trespasses."

*Mark 11:25 ESV*

**37**

Forgive as quickly and completely as the Master forgave you.

*Colossians 3:13 The Message*

**38**

He is faithful and just and will forgive us our sins.

*1 John 1:9*

**39**

The LORD our God is merciful and forgiving.

*Daniel 9:9 NLT*

**40**

"Though your sins are like scarlet, they shall be as white as snow; though they are red as crimson, they shall be like wool."

*Isaiah 1:18*

**41**

You are forgiving and good, O LORD, abounding in love to all who call to You.

*Psalm 86:5*

**42**

"Be merciful. Judge not, and you shall not be judged. Condemn not, and you shall not be condemned. Forgive, and you will be forgiven."

*Luke 6:36-37 NKJV*

———————

*A good leader, they say,*

*is someone who can*

*step on your toes*

*without messing up your shine.*

Anonymous

A Leader ...

Is Humble

There is great force hidden

in a gentle command.

*George Herbert*

**43**

When pride comes, then comes disgrace,
but with humility comes wisdom.

*Proverbs 11:2*

**44**

Fear-of-God is a school in skilled living –
first you learn humility, then you experience glory.

*Proverbs 15:33 The Message*

**45**

The reward for humility and fear of the
Lord is riches and honor and life.

*Proverbs 22:4 esv*

**46**

As God's chosen people, holy and dearly
loved, clothe yourselves with compas-
sion, kindness, humility, gentleness and
patience.

*Colossians 3:12*

**47**

Do you want to be counted wise? Here's what you do: Live well, live wisely, live humbly. It's the way you live, not the way you talk, that counts.

*James 3:13 The Message*

**48**

Be completely humble and gentle; be patient, bearing with one another in love.

*Ephesians 4:2*

**49**

Clothe yourselves, all of you, with humility toward one another, for "God opposes the proud but gives grace to the humble."

*1 Peter 5:5 ESV*

**50**

He guides the humble in what is right and teaches them His way.

*Psalm 25:9*

**51**

"For whoever humbles himself will be exalted."

*Matthew 23:12*

**52**

Haughtiness goes before destruction; humility precedes honor.

*Proverbs 18:12* NLT

---

*A person doing his or her*
*best becomes a natural leader,*
*just by example.*

Joe DiMaggio

A Leader ...

Perseveres In
Tough Times

═══════════════════════

Do not follow

where the path may lead.

Go instead where there is no

path and leave a trail.

*Harold R. McAlindon*

═══════════════════════

**53**

Be strong and immovable. Always work enthusiastically for the Lord, for you know that nothing you do for the Lord is ever useless.

*1 Corinthians 15:58 NLT*

**54**

Be strong and do not let your hands be weak, for your work shall be rewarded!

*2 Chronicles 15:7 NKJV*

**55**

Let us also lay aside every weight, and sin which clings so closely, and let us run with endurance the race that is set before us, looking to Jesus, the founder and perfecter of our faith.

*Hebrews 12:1-2 ESV*

**56**

"Everyone who endures to the end will be saved."

*Matthew 10:22 NLT*

## 57

"Keep on asking, and you will receive what you ask for. Keep on seeking, and you will find. Keep on knocking, and the door will be opened to you."

*Matthew 7:7 NLT*

## 58

We also rejoice in our sufferings, because we know that suffering produces perseverance; perseverance, character; and character, hope. And hope does not disappoint us.

*Romans 5:3-5*

## 59

My brethren, count it all joy when you fall into various trials, knowing that the testing of your faith produces patience. But let patience have its perfect work, that you may be perfect and complete, lacking nothing.

*James 1:2-4 NKJV*

**60**

Blessed is the man who perseveres under trial, because when he has stood the test, he will receive the crown of life that God has promised to those who love Him.

*James 1:12*

**61**

Let us hold tightly without wavering to the hope we affirm, for God can be trusted to keep His promise.

*Hebrews 10:23 NLT*

---

*The first order of things to be changed is me, the leader. After I consider how hard it is to change myself, then I will understand the challenge of trying to change others. This is the ultimate test of leadership.*

John Maxwell

A Leader ...

Relies on God
for Ability

The test of character is

having the ability to

meet challenges.

*Walter Annenberg*

**62**

"Everything is possible for him who believes."

*Mark 9:23*

**63**

I can do all things through Christ who strengthens me.

*Philippians 4:13 NKJV*

**64**

The Sovereign LORD is my strength; He makes my feet like the feet of a deer, He enables me to go on the heights.

*Habakkuk 3:19*

**65**

"For everyone to whom much is given, from him much will be required; and to whom much has been committed, of him they will ask the more."

*Luke 12:48 NKJV*

**66**

"My grace is sufficient for you, for My power is made perfect in weakness."

*2 Corinthians 12:9 ESV*

**67**

"Not by might nor by power, but by My Spirit," says the LORD Almighty.

*Zechariah 4:6*

**68**

Trust in the Lord with all your heart, and do not lean on your own understanding. In all your ways acknowledge Him, and He will make straight your paths.

*Proverbs 3:5-6 ESV*

**69**

The LORD is good to those whose hope is in Him, to the one who seeks Him.

*Lamentations 3:25*

### 70

Remember the LORD your God. He is the one who gives you power to be successful.

*Deuteronomy 8:18 NLT*

### 71

"So do not fear, for I am with you; do not be dismayed, for I am your God. I will strengthen you and help you; I will uphold you with My righteous right hand."

*Isaiah 41:10*

---

*A leader is great, not because*
*of his or her power,*
*but because of his or her ability*
*to empower others.*

John Maxwell

# When You

## Need ...

When You Need ...

Confidence

No man has a right

to expect others to display

confidence in him if he has

no confidence in himself.

*Roy L. Smith*

**72**

For the LORD will be your confidence, and will keep your foot from being caught.

*Proverbs 3:26 NKJV*

**73**

Blessed is the man who trusts in the LORD, whose confidence is in Him.

*Jeremiah 17:7*

**74**

God has not given us a spirit of fear, but of power and of love and of a sound mind.

*2 Timothy 1:7 NKJV*

**75**

This is the confidence we have in approaching God: that if we ask anything according to His will, He hears us.

*1 John 5:14*

### 76

"In Me you may have peace. In the world you will have tribulation. But take heart; I have overcome the world."

*John 16:33 ESV*

### 77

The LORD keeps watch over you as you come and go, both now and forever.

*Psalm 121:8 NLT*

### 78

"Everything is possible for him who believes."

*Mark 9:23*

### 79

"Ask, and it will be given to you; seek, and you will find; knock, and it will be opened to you. For everyone who asks receives, and the one who seeks finds, and to the one who knocks it will be opened."

*Matthew 7:7-8 ESV*

**80**

I am confident I will see the LORD's goodness while I am here in the land of the living. Wait patiently for the LORD. Be brave and courageous. Yes, wait patiently for the LORD.

*Psalm 27:13 NLT*

---

*You gain strength, courage*
*and confidence*
*by every experience*
*in which you really stop*
*to look fear in the face.*
*You must do the things*
*you think you cannot do.*

Eleanor Roosevelt

When You Need ...

Encouragement

Never doubt that

a small group of thoughtful,

committed citizens can

change the world. Indeed it is

the only thing that ever has.

*Margaret Mead*

**81**

Those who trust in the LORD will find new strength. They will soar high on wings like eagles. They will run and not grow weary. They will walk and not faint.

*Isaiah 40:31 NLT*

**82**

"For I know the plans I have for you," declares the LORD, "plans to prosper you and not to harm you, plans to give you hope and a future."

*Jeremiah 29:11*

**83**

So let's not get tired of doing what is good. At just the right time we will reap a harvest of blessing if we don't give up.

*Galatians 6:9 NLT*

**84**

To the one who pleases Him, God has given wisdom and knowledge and joy.

*Ecclesiastes 2:26 ESV*

**85**

The LORD your God in your midst, the Mighty One, will save; He will rejoice over you with gladness, He will quiet you with His love, He will rejoice over you with singing.

*Zephaniah 3:17 NKJV*

**86**

May our Lord Jesus Christ Himself and God our Father, who loved us and by His grace gave us eternal encouragement and good hope, encourage your hearts and strengthen you in every good deed and word.

*2 Thessalonians 2:16-17*

**87**

For we are His workmanship, created in Christ Jesus for good works, which God prepared beforehand that we should walk in them.

*Ephesians 2:10 NKJV*

When You Need ...

Guidance

Hang this question up

in your houses,

"What Would Jesus Do?"

and then think of another,

"How Would Jesus Do It?"

For what Jesus would do,

and how He would do it,

may always stand as

the best guide to us.

*Charles H. Spurgeon*

**88**

The LORD will guide you always.

*Isaiah 58:11*

**89**

"Call to Me and I will answer you, and will tell you great and hidden things that you have not known."

*Jeremiah 33:3 ESV*

**90**

The LORD says, "I will guide you along the best pathway for your life. I will advise you and watch over you."

*Psalm 32:8 NLT*

**91**

In all your ways acknowledge Him, and He shall direct your paths.

*Proverbs 3:6 NKJV*

**92**

He guides me along right paths, bringing honor to His name.

*Psalm 23:3 NLT*

**93**

May the Lord direct your hearts into God's love and Christ's perseverance.

*2 Thessalonians 3:5*

**94**

The laws of the LORD are true; each one is fair. They are a warning to your servant, a great reward for those who obey them.

*Psalm 19:9, 11 NLT*

**95**

"I know the plans I have for you," declares the LORD, "plans to prosper you and not to harm you, plans to give you hope and a future."

*Jeremiah 29:11*

**96**

All Scripture is breathed out by God and profitable for teaching, for reproof, for correction, and for training in righteousness, that the man of God may be competent, equipped for every good work.

*2 Timothy 3:16-17 ESV*

**97**

Your commandments give me understanding. Your word is a lamp to guide my feet and a light for my path.

*Psalm 119:104-105 NLT*

---

*The real leader*

*has no need to lead –*

*he is content to point the way.*

Henry Miller

When You Need ...

Inspiration

---

# Dare to be remarkable!

*Anonymous*

---

### 98

Do not despise these small beginnings, for the LORD rejoices to see the work begin.

*Zechariah 4:10 NLT*

### 99

Whatever things are true, whatever things are noble, whatever things are just, whatever things are pure, whatever things are lovely, whatever things are of good report, if there is any virtue and if there is anything praiseworthy – meditate on these things.

*Philippians 4:8 NKJV*

### 100

If you call out for insight and raise your voice for understanding, if you seek it like silver and search for it as for hidden treasures, then you will find the knowledge of God.

*Proverbs 2:3-5 ESV*

### 101

Look to the LORD and His strength; seek His face always.

*1 Chronicles 16:11*

### 102

I say to myself, "The LORD is my inheritance; therefore, I will hope in Him!"

*Lamentations 3:24 NLT*

### 103

We fix our eyes not on what is seen, but on what is unseen. For what is seen is temporary, but what is unseen is eternal.

*2 Corinthians 4:18*

### 104

We have received God's Spirit (not the world's spirit), so we can know the wonderful things God has freely given us.

*1 Corinthians 2:12 NLT*

When You Need ...

Patience

Patience is power;

with time and patience

the mulberry leaf

becomes silk.

*Chinese Proverb*

### 105

The Lord is not slow in keeping His promise, as some understand slowness. He is patient with you.

*2 Peter 3:9*

### 106

Rejoice in our confident hope. Be patient in trouble, and keep on praying.

*Romans 12:12 NLT*

### 107

Hope that is seen is no hope at all. Who hopes for what he already has? But if we hope for what we do not yet have, we wait for it patiently.

*Romans 8:24-25*

### 108

With patience a ruler may be persuaded.

*Proverbs 25:15 ESV*

## 109

The LORD is good to those who depend on Him, to those who search for Him. So it is good to wait quietly for salvation from the LORD.

*Lamentations 3:25 NLT*

## 110

Rest in the LORD, and wait patiently for Him.

*Psalm 37:7 NKJV*

## 111

We pray that you will be strengthened with all His glorious power so you will have all the endurance and patience you need.

*Colossians 1:11 NLT*

## 112

Love is patient.

*1 Corinthians 13:4*

## 113

The longer we wait, the more joyful our expectancy.

*Romans 8:25 The Message*

## 114

I waited patiently for the LORD; He turned to me and heard my cry.

*Psalm 40:1*

## 115

For the vision is yet for an appointed time; but at the end it will speak, and it will not lie. Though it tarries, wait for it; because it will surely come, it will not tarry.

*Habakkuk 2:3 NKJV*

---

*Patience is the companion of wisdom.*

St. Augustine

When You Need ...

To Unwind

What is this life if,

full of care, we have no time

to stand and stare.

*W. H. Davies*

## 116

The LORD makes me lie down in green pastures, He leads me beside quiet waters, He restores my soul.

*Psalm 23:2-3*

## 117

Give all your worries and cares to God, for He cares about you.

*1 Peter 5:7 NLT*

## 118

The LORD is my light and my salvation – whom shall I fear? The LORD is the stronghold of my life – of whom shall I be afraid?

*Psalm 27:1*

## 119

"Are you tired? Worn out? Come to Me. Get away with Me and you'll recover your life."

*Matthew 11:28 The Message*

**120**

My soul will be satisfied as with the richest of foods; with singing lips my mouth will praise You. Because You are my help, I sing in the shadow of Your wings.

*Psalm 63:5, 7*

**121**

Those who trust in the LORD will find new strength.

*Isaiah 40:31 NLT*

**122**

"Be still, and know that I am God."

*Psalm 46:10*

**123**

Be of good courage, and He shall strengthen your heart, all you who hope in the LORD.

*Psalm 31:24 NKJV*

When You Need ...

Unity in Your
Team

If I have seen farther

than others,

it is because

I was standing

on the shoulders

of giants.

*Isaac Newton*

## 124

May the God who gives endurance and encouragement give you a spirit of unity among yourselves as you follow Christ Jesus.

*Romans 15:5*

## 125

Live in harmony with one another.

*Romans 12:16 ESV*

## 126

A threefold cord is not quickly broken.

*Ecclesiastes 4:12 NKJV*

## 127

May the God of endurance and encouragement grant you to live in such harmony with one another, in accord with Christ Jesus, that together you may with one voice glorify the God and Father of our Lord Jesus Christ.

*Romans 15:5-6 ESV*

### 128

You must get along with each other. You must learn to be considerate of one another, cultivating a life in common.

*1 Corinthians 1:10 The Message*

### 129

Always be humble and gentle. Make every effort to keep yourselves united in the Spirit, binding yourselves together with peace.

*Ephesians 4:2-3 NLT*

### 130

Finally, all of you, live in harmony with one another; be sympathetic, love as brothers, be compassionate and humble.

*1 Peter 3:8*

### 131

How wonderful and pleasant it is when brothers live together in harmony! For harmony is as precious as the anointing oil.

*Psalm 133:1-2 NLT*

When You Need ...

Wisdom

A man should never be

ashamed to own he has

been in the wrong,

which is but saying

in other words,

that he is wiser today

than he was yesterday.

*Jonathan Swift*

### 132

"I will instruct you and teach you in the way you should go; I will counsel you and watch over you."

*Psalm 32:8*

### 133

You have received the Holy Spirit, and He lives within you, so you don't need anyone to teach you what is true. For the Spirit teaches you everything you need to know, and what He teaches is true.

*1 John 2:27 NLT*

### 134

If any of you lacks wisdom, let him ask of God, who gives to all liberally and without reproach, and it will be given to him.

*James 1:5 NKJV*

### 135

God gives wisdom, knowledge, and joy to those who please Him.

*Ecclesiastes 2:26 NLT*

**136**

Behold, You delight in truth in the inward being, and You teach me wisdom in the secret heart.

*Psalm 51:6 ESV*

**137**

The LORD gives wisdom; from His mouth come knowledge and understanding.

*Proverbs 2:6 NKJV*

**138**

It is through me, Lady Wisdom, that your life deepens, and the years of your life ripen.

*Proverbs 9:11 The Message*

**139**

Wisdom is sweet to your soul. If you find it, you will have a bright future, and your hopes will not be cut short.

*Proverbs 24:14 NLT*

# What the

# Bible Says About ...

What the

Bible Says About ...

Accomplishing
Your Goals

Though leadership may

be hard to define,

the one characteristic

common to all leaders

is the ability to

make things happen.

*Ted W. Engstrom*

### 140

I run with purpose in every step. I am not just shadowboxing. I discipline my body like an athlete, training it to do what it should.

*1 Corinthians 9:26-27 NLT*

### 141

Delight yourself in the LORD, and He will give you the desires of your heart.

*Psalm 37:4 ESV*

### 142

Your word is a lamp to my feet and a light to my path.

*Psalm 119:105 NKJV*

### 143

"Seek the Kingdom of God above all else, and live righteously, and He will give you everything you need."

*Matthew 6:33 NLT*

**144**

"For where your treasure is, there your heart will be also."

*Matthew 6:21 ESV*

**145**

All glory to God, who is able, through His mighty power at work within us, to accomplish infinitely more than what we might ask or think.

*Ephesians 3:20 NLT*

**146**

The LORD your God will bless you in all your harvest and in all the work of your hands, and your joy will be complete.

*Deuteronomy 16:15*

**147**

God is able to make all grace abound to you, that you, always having all sufficiency in all things, may have an abundance for every good work.

*2 Corinthians 9:8 NKJV*

### 148

"I will do whatever you ask in My name, so that the Son may bring glory to the Father. You may ask Me for anything in My name, and I will do it."

*John 14:13-14*

---

*The quality of a person's life is in direct opposition to their commitment to excellence, regardless of their chosen field of endeavor.*

Vincent T. Lombardi

What the

Bible Says About ...

Accountability

It is not only what we do,

but also what we do not do,

for which we are accountable.

*Molière*

### 149

Select from all the people some capable, honest men who fear God and hate bribes. Appoint them as leaders.

*Exodus 18:21 NLT*

### 150

Fools are headstrong and do what they like; wise people take advice.

*Proverbs 12:15 The Message*

### 151

"Can anyone hide himself in secret places, so I shall not see him?" says the LORD; "Do I not fill heaven and earth?"

*Jeremiah 23:24 NKJV*

### 152

A man reaps what he sows. The one who sows to please the Spirit, from the Spirit will reap eternal life.

*Galatians 6:7-8*

### 153

It's wonderful to be young! Enjoy every minute of it. Do everything you want to do; take it all in. But remember that you must give an account to God for everything you do.

*Ecclesiastes 11:9 NLT*

### 154

Don't let evil get the best of you; get the best of evil by doing good.

*Romans 12:21 The Message*

### 155

The godly are directed by honesty.

*Proverbs 11:5 NLT*

### 156

So join the company of good men and women, keep your feet on the tried and true paths.

*Proverbs 2:20 The Message*

**157**

God will judge us for everything we do, including every secret thing, whether good or bad.

*Ecclesiastes 12:14 NLT*

**158**

Nothing in all creation is hidden from God's sight. Everything is uncovered and laid bare before the eyes of Him to whom we must give account.

*Hebrews 4:13*

---

*In matters of style,*
*swim with the current;*
*in matters of principle,*
*stand like a rock.*

Thomas Jefferson

What the

Bible Says About ...

Contentment

True contentment

is the power

of getting out

of any situation

all that there is in it.

*G. K. Chesterton*

### 159

I have learned to be content whatever the circumstances. I have learned the secret of being content in any and every situation, whether well fed or hungry, whether living in plenty or in want.

*Philippians 4:11-12*

### 160

True godliness with contentment is itself great wealth.

*1 Timothy 6:6 NLT*

### 161

"Because he loves Me," says the LORD, "I will rescue him; I will protect him, for he acknowledges My name."

*Psalm 91:14*

### 162

You will keep in perfect peace all who trust in You, all whose thoughts are fixed on You!

*Isaiah 26:3 NLT*

## 163

The fear of the LORD leads to life: the one rests content, untouched by trouble.

*Proverbs 19:23*

## 164

You open Your hand and satisfy the desires of every living thing.

*Psalm 145:16*

## 165

We brought nothing into this world, and it is certain we can carry nothing out. And having food and clothing, with these we shall be content.

*1 Timothy 6:7-8 NKJV*

## 166

And I – in righteousness I will see Your face; when I awake, I will be satisfied with seeing Your likeness.

*Psalm 17:15*

### 167

Keep your life free from love of money, and be content with what you have, for He has said, "I will never leave you nor forsake you."

*Hebrews 13:5*

### 168

The one who blesses others is abundantly blessed; those who help others are helped. Blessings on all who play fair and square!

*Proverbs 11:25-26 The Message*

### 169

"Whoever drinks of the water that I will give him will never be thirsty forever. The water that I will give him will become in him a spring of water welling up to eternal life."

*John 4:14 ESV*

What the
Bible Says About ...

Failure

It is nobler to try

something and fail than

to try nothing and succeed.

The result may be the

same but you won't be.

We always grow more

through defeats

than victories.

*Anonymous*

### 170

For we do not have a high priest who is unable to sympathize with our weaknesses. Let us then with confidence draw near to the throne of grace, that we may receive mercy and find grace to help in time of need.

*Hebrews 4:15-16 ESV*

### 171

Generous in love – God, give grace! Huge in mercy – wipe out my bad record. Scrub away my guilt, soak out my sins in Your laundry.

*Psalm 51:1-2 The Message*

### 172

Because of the LORD's great love we are not consumed, for His compassions never fail. They are new every morning; great is Your faithfulness.

*Lamentations 3:22-23*

### 173

"My grace is all you need. My power works best in weakness." So now I am glad to boast about my weakness, so that the power of Christ can work through me.

*2 Corinthians 12:9 NLT*

### 174

Thanks be to God, who always leads us in triumphal procession in Christ.

*2 Corinthians 2:14*

### 175

We can make our plans, but the LORD determines our steps.

*Proverbs 16:9 NLT*

### 176

The LORD upholds all those who fall and lifts up all who are bowed down.

*Psalm 145:14*

### 177

I take limitations in stride, and with good cheer. I just let Christ take over! And so the weaker I get, the stronger I become.

*2 Corinthians 12:10 The Message*

### 178

We don't look at the troubles we can see now; rather, we fix our gaze on things that cannot be seen. For the things we see now will soon be gone, but the things we cannot see will last forever.

*2 Corinthians 4:18 NLT*

### 179

Therefore, since through God's mercy we have this ministry, we do not lose heart. On the contrary, by setting forth the truth plainly we commend ourselves to every man's conscience in the sight of God.

*2 Corinthians 4:1-2*

What the

Bible Says About ...

Leadership

If your actions inspire

others to dream more,

learn more, do more

and become more,

you are a leader.

*John Quincy Adams*

### 180

Don't push your way to the front; don't sweet-talk your way to the top. Put yourself aside, and help others get ahead. Don't be obsessed with getting your own advantage. Forget yourselves long enough to lend a helping hand.

*Philippians 2:2-4 The Message*

### 181

Without wise leadership, a nation falls; there is safety in having many advisers.

*Proverbs 11:14 NLT*

### 182

Make friends with nobodies; don't be the great somebody.

*Romans 12:16 The Message*

### 183

Get the truth and never sell it; also get wisdom, discipline, and good judgment.

*Proverbs 23:23 NLT*

**184**

Good counsel and common sense are my characteristics; I am both Insight and the Virtue to live it out.

*Proverbs 8:14 The Message*

**185**

You guide me with Your counsel, leading me to a glorious destiny.

*Psalm 73:24 NLT*

**186**

For am I now seeking the approval of man, or of God? Or am I trying to please man? If I were still trying to please man, I would not be a servant of Christ.

*Galatians 1:10 ESV*

**187**

If you listen to constructive criticism, you will be at home among the wise.

*Proverbs 15:31 NLT*

**188**

The mouth of the righteous man utters wisdom. The law of his God is in his heart; his feet do not slip.

*Psalm 37:30-31*

**189**

Work hard and become a leader; be lazy and become a slave. Worry weighs a person down; an encouraging word cheers a person up.

*Proverbs 12:24-25 NLT*

———————————————

*Leaders have two characteristics:*
*First they are going somewhere, and*
*second they are able to persuade*
*other people to go with them.*

John Maxwell

What the

Bible Says About ...

Troubles

All our difficulties

are only platforms

for the manifestation

of God's grace,

power and love.

*Hudson Taylor*

### 190

A thousand may fall at your side, ten thousand at your right hand, but it will not come near you.

*Psalm 91:7 ESV*

### 191

"Peace I leave with you; My peace I give you. I do not give to you as the world gives. Do not let your hearts be troubled and do not be afraid."

*John 14:27*

### 192

God is our refuge and strength, a very present help in trouble.

*Psalm 46:1 NKJV*

### 193

If God is for us, who can be against us? He who did not spare His own Son, but gave Him up for us all – how will He not also graciously give us all things?

*Romans 8:31-32*

### 194

Wait for the LORD; be strong and take heart and wait for the LORD.

*Psalm 27:14*

### 195

I will lift up my eyes to the hills – from whence comes my help? My help comes from the LORD, who made heaven and earth.

*Psalm 121:1-2 NKJV*

### 196

I will be glad and rejoice in Your unfailing love, for You have seen my troubles, and You care about the anguish of my soul.

*Psalm 31:7 NLT*

### 197

The LORD is good, a stronghold in the day of trouble; and He knows those who trust in Him.

*Nahum 1:7 NKJV*